THE FROG *who* WOULDN'T LAUGH

Written by CECILIA EGAN

Illustrated by ELIZABETH ALGER

Pancake
Press

ISBN: 0 3303 5810 3
First published in Australia 1996 by Pancake Press
an imprint of Pan Macmillan Australia Pty. Ltd.
St Martins Tower, 31 Market Street
Sydney NSW 2000

©1996 Pan Macmillan Australia Pty. Ltd.

Colour Separations by Litho Platemakers
Printed in Australia by Southbank Book.

National Library of Australia
cataloguing-in-publication data available:
398.2450994

FOREWORD

These wonderful legends of the native Australians have been adapted to be read and understood by children. Young ones too, can gain an insight into the rich and complex culture that existed for tens of thousands of years before Europeans landed.

The stories are not intended to be exact replicas of the original tales, but attempt to convey the narrative in a manner to which children can relate.

Titles in this series:

White Clay and the Giant Kangaroos
The Frog Who Wouldn't Laugh
The Willy-Willy and the Ant
Magic Colours

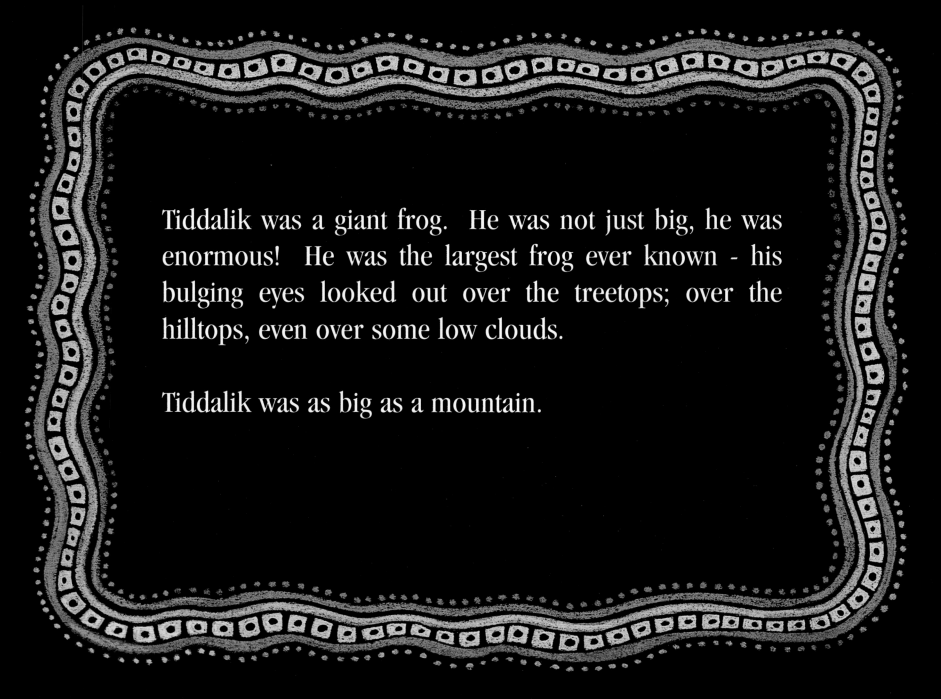

Tiddalik was a giant frog. He was not just big, he was enormous! He was the largest frog ever known - his bulging eyes looked out over the treetops; over the hilltops, even over some low clouds.

Tiddalik was as big as a mountain.

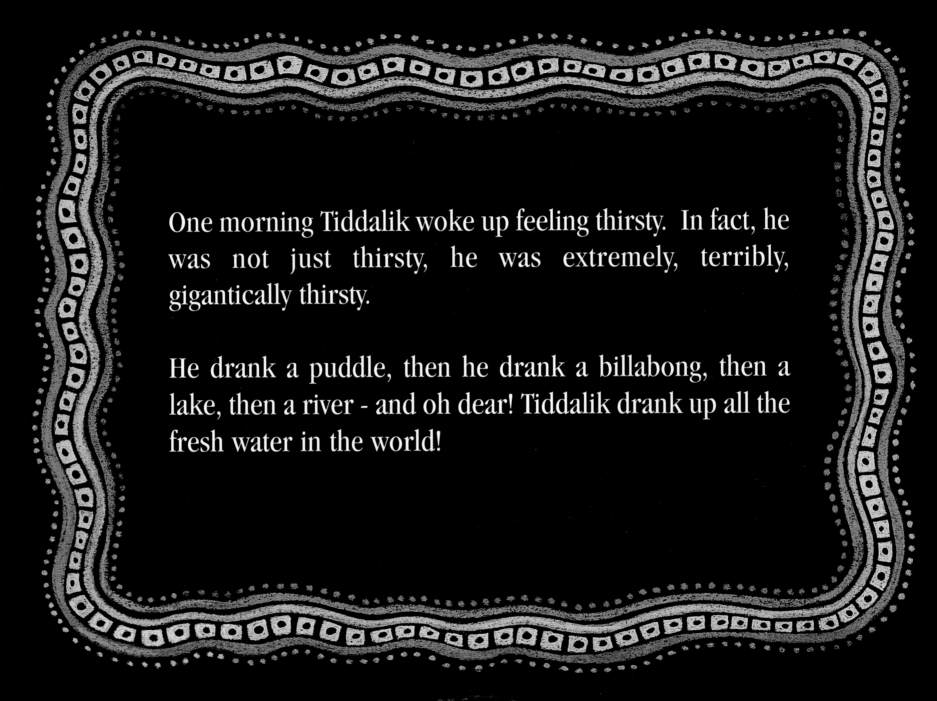

One morning Tiddalik woke up feeling thirsty. In fact, he was not just thirsty, he was extremely, terribly, gigantically thirsty.

He drank a puddle, then he drank a billabong, then a lake, then a river - and oh dear! Tiddalik drank up all the fresh water in the world!

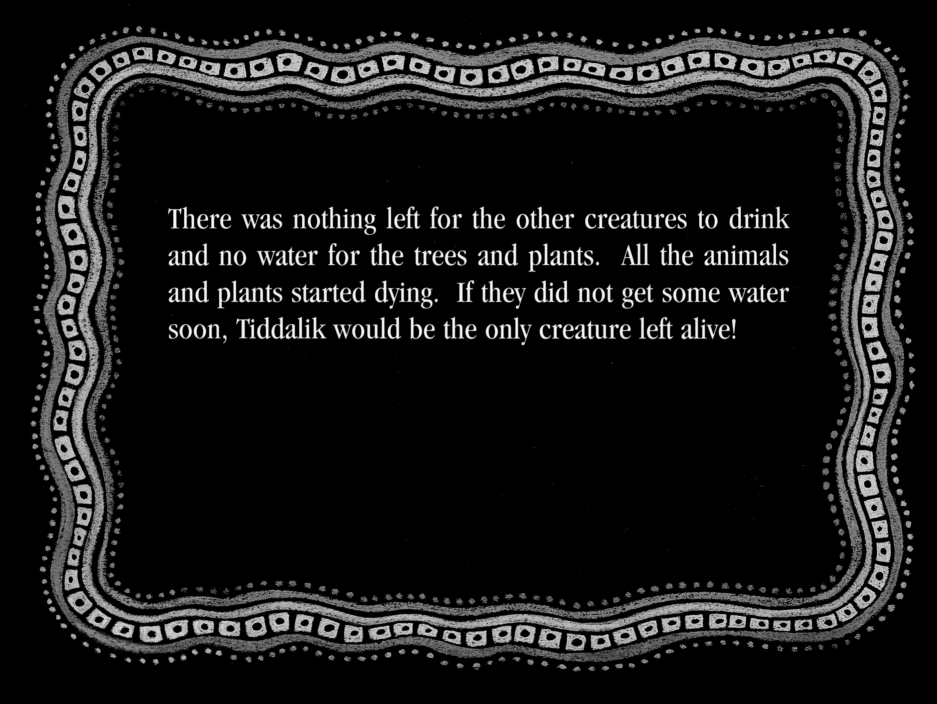

There was nothing left for the other creatures to drink and no water for the trees and plants. All the animals and plants started dying. If they did not get some water soon, Tiddalik would be the only creature left alive!

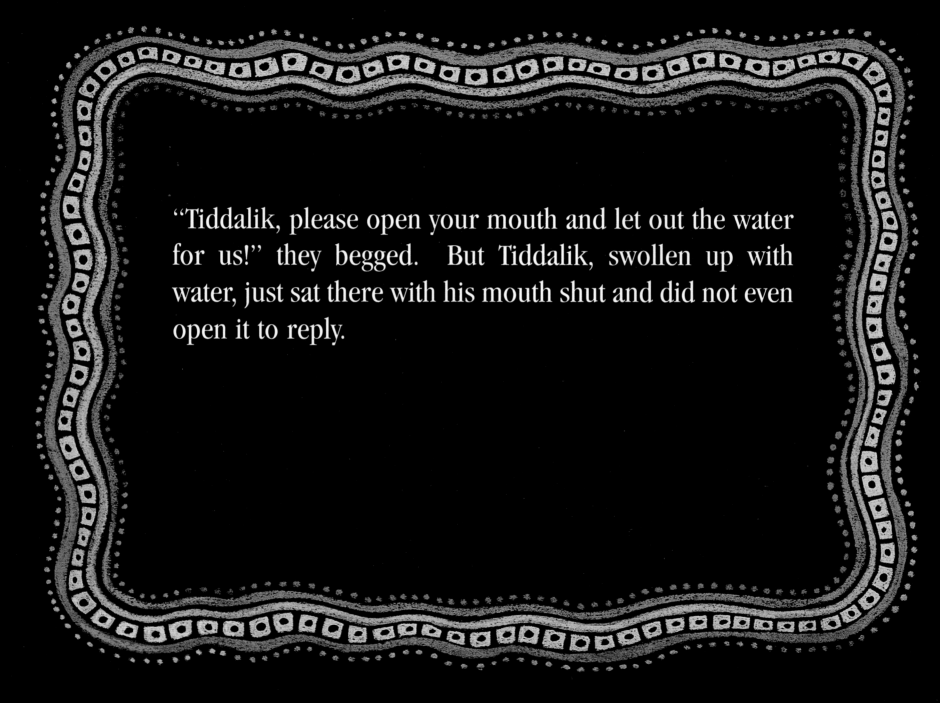

"Tiddalik, please open your mouth and let out the water for us!" they begged. But Tiddalik, swollen up with water, just sat there with his mouth shut and did not even open it to reply.

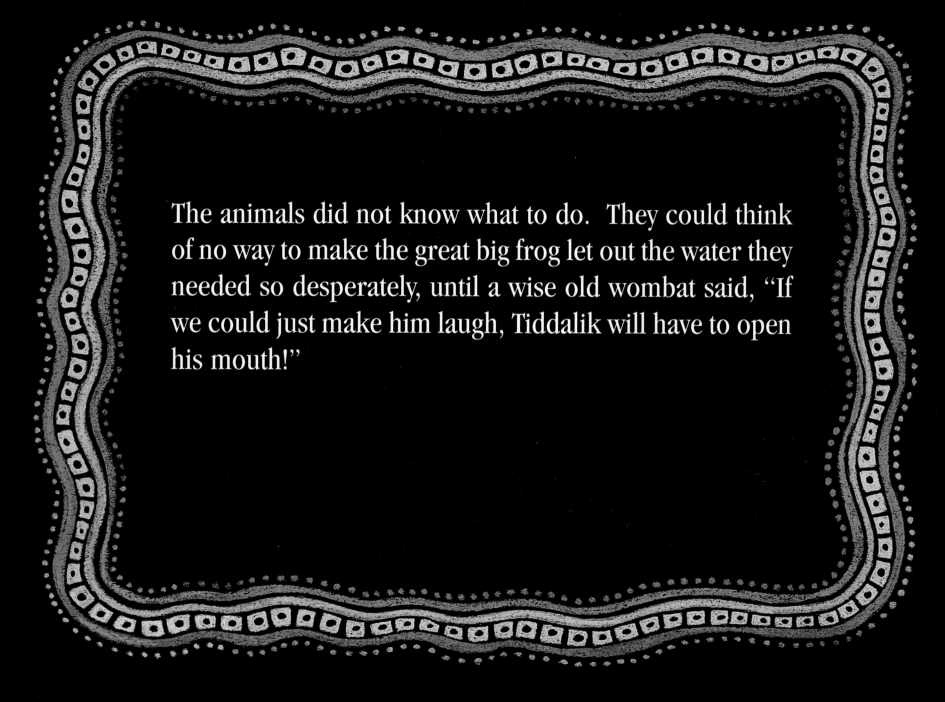

The animals did not know what to do. They could think of no way to make the great big frog let out the water they needed so desperately, until a wise old wombat said, "If we could just make him laugh, Tiddalik will have to open his mouth!"

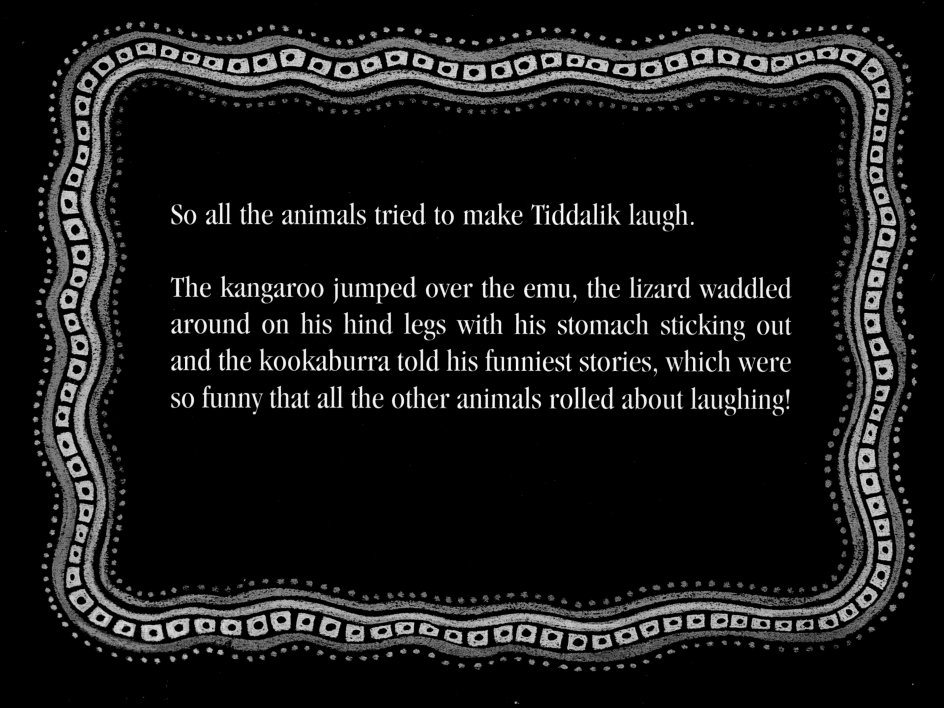

So all the animals tried to make Tiddalik laugh.

The kangaroo jumped over the emu, the lizard waddled around on his hind legs with his stomach sticking out and the kookaburra told his funniest stories, which were so funny that all the other animals rolled about laughing!

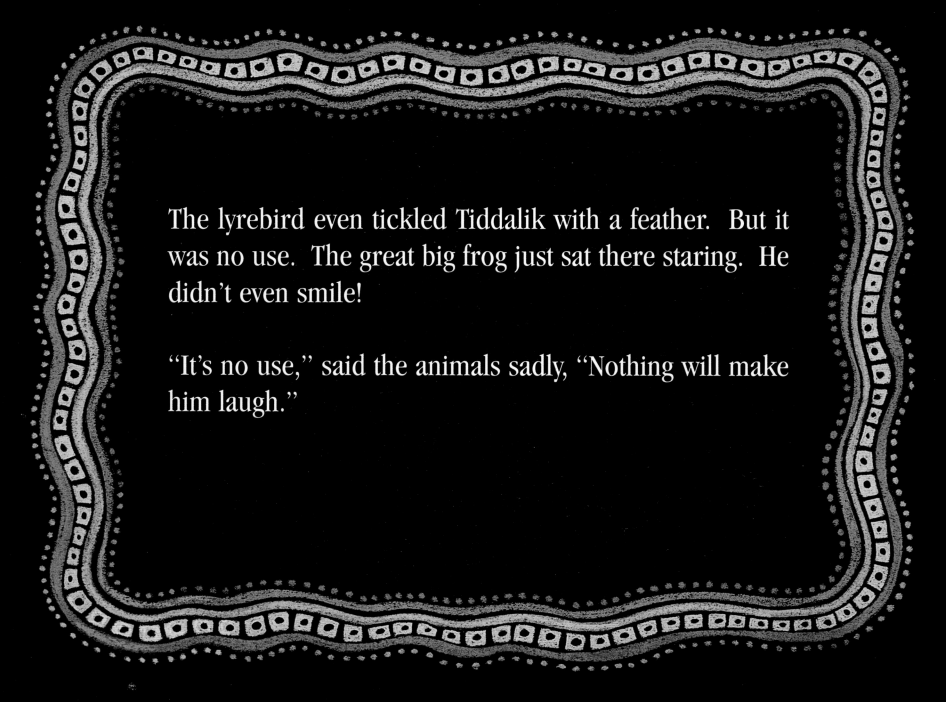

The lyrebird even tickled Tiddalik with a feather. But it was no use. The great big frog just sat there staring. He didn't even smile!

"It's no use," said the animals sadly, "Nothing will make him laugh."

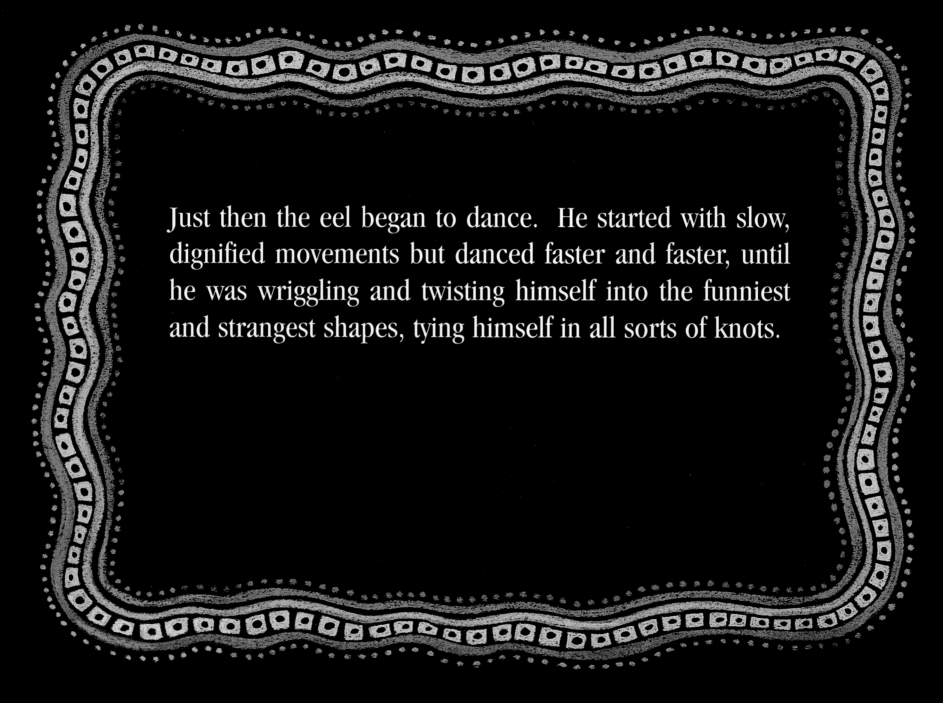

Just then the eel began to dance. He started with slow, dignified movements but danced faster and faster, until he was wriggling and twisting himself into the funniest and strangest shapes, tying himself in all sorts of knots.

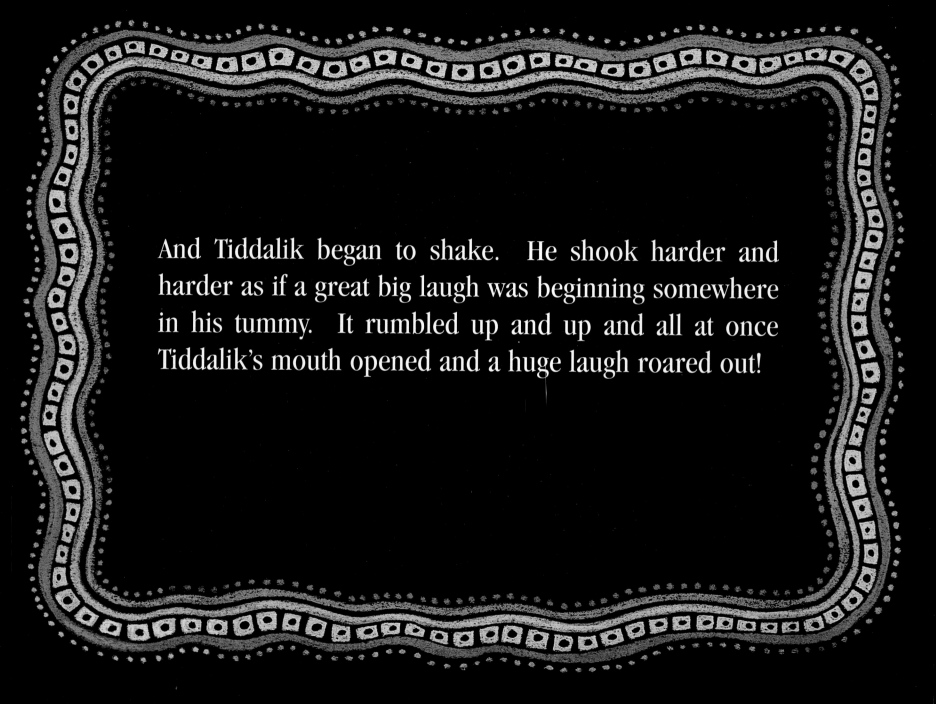

And Tiddalik began to shake. He shook harder and harder as if a great big laugh was beginning somewhere in his tummy. It rumbled up and up and all at once Tiddalik's mouth opened and a huge laugh roared out!

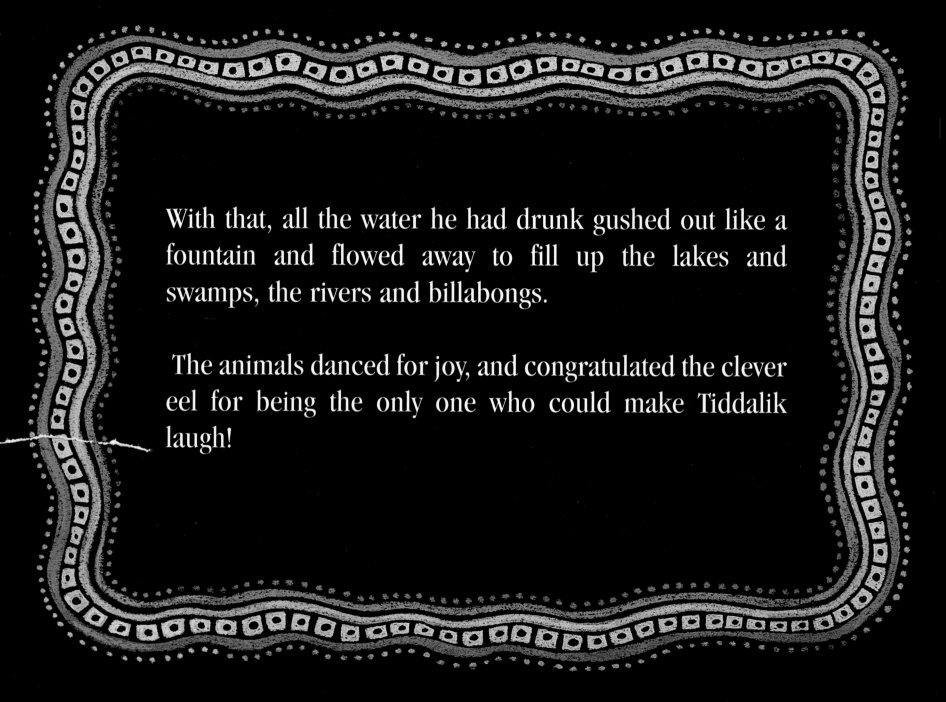

With that, all the water he had drunk gushed out like a fountain and flowed away to fill up the lakes and swamps, the rivers and billabongs.

The animals danced for joy, and congratulated the clever eel for being the only one who could make Tiddalik laugh!